i c e   c r a d l e
a portrait of the baby harp seal

Rei Ohara

Takarajima Books

A Harp Seal mother and baby sniff each other to confirm that they are related.

They spend only two weeks together, and this is their closest moment.

The color of a newborn pup is yellowish, tinged by the mother's birth fluids.

Soon a baby seal turns pure snow white, bleached by sunshine and snow.

A new-born seal with its umbilical cord still attached. It will be discarded naturally over the next few days while crawling on the ice fields.

Staying on the drift ice is the safest haven for the unprotected baby

seal. They roll over and over, enjoying their paradise without threat.

When a snow storm hits the drift ice, the temperature sometimes drops to -50 degrees centigrade. Despite the severe conditions, baby seals brave the cold.

These happy first two weeks pass quickly—mother seals will

soon leave for the Northern seas, abandoning their pups.

Every March, hundreds of thousands of mother harp seals give birth to white, furry pups. It is still winter at this stage, with temperatures sometimes as low as -20 F; life for a newborn harp seal has always begun on the cold, windy surface of the sea ice.

Off the eastern coast of Canada 600,000 pups are born each year in one of two main herds. The largest herd is found off the coast of Labrador, and a smaller one is near the tiny Magdalen Islands in the Gulf of the St. Lawrence River.

For two or three months before giving birth, a mother harp seal spends her days eating as much as she possibly can, feeding on a dozen different kinds of fish, as well as krill, shrimp and other marine invertebates. At the end of this great feast, mother seals are the fattest they will be all year, but with good reason—once the baby is born, its mother will not eat for several weeks while feeding a steady supply of rich milk for which a thick layer of fat serves as an energy reserve.

The birth of a harp seal happens very fast; usually it's all over in less than a minute. Harp seals rarely have more than a single pup, since a mother could never supply enough milk. Moments after a pup is born, the mother spins around on the ice and sniffs her new offspring. It's very important for her to memorize the smell and sound of her own pup, since a mother

seal will only provide milk for her own and sometimes there may be three or four hungry seal pups lying around a hole in the ice waiting to be nursed.

A new born is called a *yellowcoat* because of its straw-colored fur, stained from the birth fluids, which gradually fades in the sunshine in three or four days. The fluffy bleached pup is then called a *whitecoat*. The pup grows very, very fast. At birth, a harp seal weighs 22 pounds, is skinny, and its head looks disproportionately large. By the time the pup is just two weeks old it has ballooned to almost 75 pounds, and looks like a stuffed sausage with a black nose and whiskers stuck on one end.

Pups are able to grow so quickly because their mother's milk contains as much as 60 percent fat, fifteen times more fat than cow's milk—like a very thick warm milkshake. Suckling six or seven times every day in the first few weeks of its life, it's little wonder that a baby seals get fat so fast.

While only nursing for about an hour every day, whitecoats spend most of their spare time sleeping. Newborn seal pups have sharp, well-developed front claws which they use to wiggle and crawl around the surface of the ice to avoid the wind and cold. Often a young pup will sleep in the shelter of a snowdrift or a ice ridge, or wedge itself into a crevice. Sometimes the pup may sleep in the same spot over and over

again so that its body heat actually melts a depression in the ice shaped like a cradle.

By the time a whitecoat is a week old it has a thick layer of insulating blubber and doesn't mind the wind and cold of its 'nursery'. It loses so little body heat that snow doesn't melt on the pup's fur and often ends up covering it with a blanket of new-fallen flakes.

The leisurely life of feeding and snoozing ends abruptly when the seal pup is just 12 days old. Suddenly, one day, mother disappears and never comes back again. The pup eventually accepts the departure, and is called a *ragged-jacket*. When the shedding is complete it looks sleek and healthy in a shiny new silver-grey pelt with large black spots - now called a *beater*.

The freshly independent seal has probably never gone into the water, and has not eaten since its mother abandoned it. Hunger eventually forces the young animal into the water to search for food. A seal's first efforts to swim may be a little clumsy, and young seals are called beaters because of the way they splash about with their flippers trying to learn. Nonetheless, in no time they are catching small shrimp and krill.

What happens to the mother seal once she weans the pups? In most cases, she joins up with an adult male seal, mates with him, and becomes pregnant again. By this time the sea ice has begun to melt and break up, and soon afterwards all of the seals start to migrate north to Greenland. Most of the adult seals will spend the summer and early autumn in the Arctic before they return south again. There, a new batch of pups will be born, starting the annual cycle once more.

Young harp seal pups are adorable, with a beautiful coat of fur over their thick layer of blubber. Hunting of young harp seals for their fur coat and fat began in Canada over 200 years ago. In the mid 1800s, as many as 300 ships, carrying 12,000 men, were hunting whitecoats off the eastern coast of the country. In a single season, the hunters might kill over half-a-million seals. The seal harvest continued like this for over a hundred years, and millions of whitecoats were killed for their pelts and fat.

In the early 1960s the annual seal hunt began to attract the attention of the general public. People protested, and in March 1982 the European Parliament voted to ban the trade of all harp seal skins. The seal hunt collapsed.

These days, every year, hundreds of visitors fly to the Magdalen Islands and then travel by helicopter to the sea ice to photograph the seal pups. At least for now, the seal lovers have won the war for the whitecoats.

Wayne Lynch

ACKNOWLEDGMENTS

I express my sincere gratitude to the people of the Magdalen Islands (Îles-de-la madeleine). This book is a tribute to their courageous attempt to coexist with baby seals. I especially thank André Bourque, who initiated the baby seal observation with the islanders, Émile Richard and staff of the Château Madelinot hotel, Léonard Chevrier and other special guides on the ice, Roger Simon (Federal Fisheries and Oceans), Serge Solomon (PESPEC Foundation) and Claude Richard (Director of Tourism). I also thank the eminent biologists who meet at the Magdalen Islands each year, Kit M. Kovacs, Mike Hammil and Ronald Greendale, whose expertise was invaluable. And finally, I thank those who worked so diligently towards the book's publication: Kenichiro Tominaga (Japanese Editor), Sanae Yanai (Art Director), Akihiko Miyanaga (English Language Editor), Kazaki Kiriya (Designer, English Edition), and my photographic colleague Wayne Lynch who wrote the beautiful introduction.

Takarajima Books
200 Varick Street New York, NY 10014
Tel: (212) 675-1944
Fax: (212) 255-5731

Art Director: Sanae Yanai (plus i LIMITED)
Designer: Kazaki Kiriya

The staff at Takarajima Books for *Ice Cradle: A Portrait of the Baby Harp Seal* is:
Akihiko Miyanaga, Publisher
Kiyotaka Yaguchi, Assistant Publisher

ISBN: 1-883489-15-6

Library of Congress Card Number: 95-060614

Printed and bound by Toppan Printing Co., (Shenzhen) Ltd., China